Wouldacouldashoulda

Rapid Results
No Excuses

Margaret Rudgard Bradley, Ph.D.

Wouldacouldashoulda

ISBN: 978-0-9916434-0-0

Table of Contents

Wouldacouldashoulda

"Productivity is way up. Our department is producing 35% more mistakes, 42% more excuses and 28% more scapegoats."

"I attribute my success to
this - I never gave or took
any excuse."

Florence Nightingale

> ## "There are only two choices; make progress or make excuses."
>
> Ellen Mikesell

No More Wouldacouldashoulda: A Personal Case History

I was afraid I was going to wait until pigs flew before I wrote a book. Then I ran out of excuses.

After a long and happy career as a graduate student, I accepted a job at a subsidiary of a 200,000-employee company. I was hired to create a program that would quickly boost the number of women in senior management. At the time there were three. This was the late 1970's.

Before I started, the president told me that my goal was to get my picture on the cover of *Fortune* magazine with an accompanying feature story about the program and its impact. With great enthusiasm for the task, I left family and friends and moved 800 miles to join the organization. On my first day at work, I was told the initiative had been cancelled. Male employees had protested that they didn't want to be excluded from any fast-track program.

It turned out to be good news for me. My focus immediately changed to finding ways to identify and launch high potentials, regardless of gender. I've been working on programs that help leaders rapidly reach their potential ever since.

That job led to this book. It just took a while. About 34 years.

I didn't have the time. I had lots of other responsibilities. I was caring for elderly parents. I didn't know how. I couldn't afford to be away from my business. I didn't have the support I needed. I wasn't prepared to make big changes. Life was pretty good the way it was. I was worried that success would require lots of travel. I lacked computer skills.

The list went on and on. Lots of excuses. No action.

This book could be a case study on how to harness the power of excuses in order to create the energy and insights needed to be successful. It's a collection of strategies tested in the real world – by me, by the tens of thousands of participants in seminars I've taught, and by the leaders I've interviewed.

Flannery O'Connor once gave advice that motivated me to write this book. She pointed out that anyone who survived childhood has enough information to write for the rest of his or her life. It occurred to me that someone who has survived a career that spanned jobs in big corporations and years as an entrepreneur has lots of data others might find useful. What works and what doesn't? What makes a new leader effective instantly? How can someone significantly increase his or her professional impact? What makes a person stand out for the right reasons? Which principles of applied psychology can make work life better?

My final push came from sources that surprised me. A couple of people I had not heard from in decades called me recently and told me that my workshops had a lasting impact on them. One seminar was *"Lose the Excuses: What Do You Really Want to Do Now that You've Grown Up?"* My former colleagues said that they still use the principles learned in that seminar to make decisions.

It occurred to me that it was time to take my own advice. What was I going to do now that I was grown up? What did I want my next five years to look like? What excuses did I need to banish?

How about you? What do you really want to do? What's holding you back?

The purpose of this book is to provide

checklists, assessments, and examples that will help leaders banish excuses that stand in the way of high performance.

I want to share what I've learned so you can save time and quickly gain a sense of accomplishment – and not take 34 years to do it.

I wish you the very highest levels of satisfaction, lots of chances to seize opportunities that pay off handsomely, and fulfillment that comes from using your strengths to achieve meaningful goals. I hope you'll start to read this book immediately and use it as a guide to achieving even greater personal and professional success right away.

> ## "There is no greater burden than great potential."
>
> Charles M. Schulz

Who Should Read This Book?

This book was written for people with high potential and lots of options. It's for leaders who want to optimize where they are now and who aspire to even greater achievements.

Check all the items listed below that are goals for you.

_____ Generate more opportunities

_____ Banish regrets

_____ Increase passion for your work (paid and volunteer)

_____ Boost energy

_____ Increase focus

_____ Overcome inertia

_____ Get out of your comfort zone

_____ Make good choices

_____ Increase job and life satisfaction

_____ Feel optimistic about your future

_____ Avoid settling

_____ Achieve excellent results

_____ Enhance your professional reputation

_____ Gain self-confidence

_____ Improve your chance of reaching goals

_____ Eliminate false starts

_____ Have outstanding achievements

_____ Be recognized for adding real value

_____ Reduce stress

_____ Foster confidence of those around you

The more items you checked, the more

likely you'll benefit from implementing the strategies covered in this book. Revisit this list after you've applied the principles of excuse management to get a "before and after" snapshot.

Wouldacouldashoulda is all about enhancing the quality of your life - on and off the job - and helping leaders leap forward.

> "Some books should be tasted, some devoured, but only a few should be chewed and digested thoroughly."
>
> Francis Bacon

How to Use
Wouldacouldashoulda

Woudacouldashoulda is a field guide to spotting and identifying excuses that stand in your way. Nothing can slow progress faster than a bevy of excuses - yours or someone else's. They often mask the real reason something doesn't get done. Or they provide a distraction that diverts energy. Or they become a habit that eats up time and money.

Few things can destroy a reputation

as completely. Colleagues don't trust you. Bosses give the best assignments to others. Staff members don't take you seriously.

Wouldacouldashoulda is meant to be a book for those who don't have time to read. A short, powerful course in excuse management. As a leader, you are a role model. And what you reward is what happens.

What's the last excuse you made? What's the last excuse you accepted without asking questions? This book contains short quizzes that provide insights into your own excuse style. And it provides practical, no-cost strategies for creating an excuse-free culture.

This is a book that is meant to be devoured and shared with your work group. Just reading it by yourself won't yield optimal results. As with any field guide, it needs to be used in the "real world." It makes an ideal handout for members of a work group - especially during a launch or orientation.

First, read it and complete the checklists and assessments by yourself. Think about how the examples apply to your work environment. Then, ask team members to do the same. You'll discover ways you can eliminate barriers to success and enjoy sustained success and satisfaction - all by managing excuses. High performance. No regrets. They're yours for asking the right questions.

> ## "Sometimes I sits and thinks, and sometimes I just sits...."
>
> A.A. Milne

Wouldacouldashoulda:
No Limits to Your Thinking

Sit, read, contemplate, and share *Wouldacouldashoulda* with your team. It's portable, short, and practical. The concepts are meant to be discussed. What's the ideal environment for your team members? Are there norms now? What are they? What should they be? How can you maintain new behaviors? Effective excuse management can increase productivity, streamline communication, and enhance job satisfaction.

The best way to get the most out of *Woudacouldashoulda* is to use it as your personal workbook. Write your ideas in the book in longhand. Research has shown that writing, not typing, produces the best results. You have a greater opportunity to think about your ideas and to apply them to your own situation.

A few years ago, managers in an Information Technology department were concerned that they were not going to have good opportunities for career growth where they were. They were tired of making excuses for staying in their comfort zones and not exploring opportunities in other companies. Their strategy for overcoming inertia and eliminating their excuses was to meet weekly and discuss Richard Bolles' book, *What Color is Your Parachute?*

The book contains a lot of exercises. They knew they could all find excuses for not actually doing them, so they formed a five-person club – CAP (Career Action Planning). They met each week to talk about insights they gained while reading the book. Each week they agreed on a new assignment. And whoever had not done the homework had to pick up the check for lunch. No excuses. No absences tolerated.

All of them are now in positions of much greater responsibility. They attribute their success to doing the exercises and discussing them.

Wouldacouldashoulda works best when you treat it like a CAP club - answer the questions and ask for input from your work group. The data you gather can be used to establish norms, facilitate communication, and get alignment on priorities. Success is streamlined. Excuses are eliminated.

Chapter 1

Excuse Assessments: Data that Will Change Your Life

"I have metal fillings in my teeth. My refrigerator magnets keep pulling me into the kitchen. That's why I can't lose weight!"

"Ninety-nine percent of the failures come from people who have the habit of making excuses."

George Washington Carver

Just Didn't Do It Inventory: How to Banish Regrets and Do the Right Things

An Analysis of Your Wouldacouldashouldas

People make excuses for what they didn't do, for what they wish they'd done, and for what they shouldn't have done. There is power in making a list of your wouldacouldashouldas and thinking about the excuses you've made for both what you have done and what you haven't.

Ten years ago, John was coordinating a job fair and an exhibitor expressed an interest in meeting with him to discuss a potential job opening that might match his interests. John didn't follow through and made an excuse to himself that he was too busy. To this day, John talks about what could have happened. "I shoulda called the recruiter when he asked me to contact him. I coulda ended up with a new job that suits me much better than the one I have now. I shoulda seized the opportunity."

Fred was approached by an executive recruiter with a lucrative opportunity. He'd established a track record of 30 years of good results in a company he liked. He accepted the new position in a different industry with a culture that was foreign to him. He no longer knew how to get things done quickly or how to get support for the changes he wanted to make. He wished he'd asked more questions before making a move. He woulda made a better choice if he had done due diligence. He coulda determined if he had the skills that woulda made him a success in the new organization. He shoulda thought beyond the lure of a bigger salary and more responsibility.

Sally was promoted to head a department. Funds were tight and she had to fight for her budget and compete with other managers for scarce dollars by making a presentation to the vice presidents. She woulda been more successful if she had not assumed this audience was like others she had spoken to in the past. She coulda avoided disappointment if she'd found a mentor. She shoulda rehearsed in front of people who could give her insights on her presentation style. She woulda gotten a bigger budget if she'd been better prepared.

> "Deciding what not to do is as important as deciding what to do."
>
> Steve Jobs

Eventually some items will probably drop off your list, and you'll stop feeling the pressure of "I shoulda" where they are concerned. Other tasks that might have been in the back of your mind will become priorities.

Use the following table to make sure you're doing the right things. It's time to let go of the action items that aren't going to take you where you want to go.

If you and your team made a list of wouldacouldashouldas for your work group, what would your analysis reveal? Are you accepting excuses on high priority items? Are you investing too much time and too many resources on low priority items?

| Wouldacouldashoulda

☑ What You Wish You Would Have Done
☑ What You Could Have Done
☑ What You Should Have Done

List as many wouldacouldshoul-das as you can. Then give each one a rating of 1–5. 1 = Low and 5 = High.	Critical to Your Success?	Benefit to the Customer?	Achievable?	Want to Do It?

Example	Critical to Your Success?	Benefit to the Customer?	Achievable?	Want to Do It?
Tasks on Wouldacouldashoula list				
Reorganize files	1	1	5	1
Create a master checklist for each speech	5	3	5	3
Design a website for a book	5	5	5	5

What are your highest priority items? Doing the right things without making excuses will speed you toward success. As Stephen Covey said, "If the ladder is not leaning against the right wall, every step we take just gets us to the wrong place faster."

Excuse Style Indicator:
An Evaluation of Your Excuse Style

What's Your Excuse Profile?

What is your attitude toward excuses? Do you see them as inevitable or as something that, if managed, leads to enhanced performance? What are the characteristics of the excuses you make? Under what circumstances do you usually make excuses? Overall, would you describe yourself as an optimist or a pessimist?

If you're aware of your attitude and how you use excuses – and what an excuse really says – you'll communicate more effectively. Misunderstandings will be greatly reduced. You'll save time and money.

We all make excuses without even thinking about what we're saying. People

"I was going to buy a copy of *'The Power of Positive Thinking'* and then I thought: What good would that do?"

Ronnie Shakes

don't make excuses out of bad intentions. Becoming aware of your own tendencies will give you useful insights. As a leader, you'll learn more about what you portray as a role model. You'll gain a clearer understanding of how your colleagues see you. And you'll be better able to set a good example.

There's no right or wrong excuse mode. The checklist below is not a sophisticated, scientific assessment. But it should yield results that will give you insights into your own preferences and those of your associates. Hopefully it will make you smile in recognition and provide a light-hearted framework to discuss the topic of excuses with others.

In the Excuse Style Indicator below, read each row and check the box that appeals to you the most. Work fast. Descriptions of each style are given after the quick assessment.

Excuse Style Indicator

In each horizontal row, check one box (A, B, or C) that describes you or your preference the best. If undecided, check the middle column. Then total the checkmarks in each column.

A	B	C
__ Policies and procedures	—	__ Loose guidelines
__ Firm expectations	—	__ Surprises are welcome
__ Hierarchical	—	__ Participative
__ Planned	—	__ Spontaneous
__ Data-driven	—	__ Imaginative
__ Existing	—	__ Created from scratch
__ Straightforward	—	__ Complex
__ Decisive	—	__ Indecisive
__ Tried and true	—	__ New and different
__ Concern for power	—	__ Concern for others
__ Little need to nurture	—	__ Nurturing
__ One task at a time	—	__ Multi-tasking
__ Well organized	—	__ Little organization
__ Focused	—	__ Distractible
__ Structured	—	__ Little structure
__ Tidy	—	__ Messy
__ Low need to refine	—	__ High need to polish
__ Ready, aim, fire	—	__ Ready, fire, aim
_____ **TOTAL**	_____ **TOTAL**	_____ **TOTAL**

Excuse Me

Which column contains the highest number? That score represents your strongest excuse style. The quotes and descriptions listed below for that style apply to your view of excuses and how you use them. If columns are within a couple of points of each other, you don't have a strong preference. Think of yourself as very adaptable.

Column A: The Excuse Conquistador

If your highest number is in Column A, you can be described as an Excuse Conquistador. You are guided by principles such as: "Plan the work. Work the plan." Your attitude is one of "Take no prisoners. Excuses will not be tolerated." You finish one thing before you move on to another.

This is a style that is familiar to me. I grew up in a Navy family. You were always expected to meet certain standards. If you said you would do something, you did it. No excuses. Ever.

It's a style that comes in handy in complex situations. A friend of mine is one of nine children. A no-excuse environment reduced the chaos in her home to manageable proportions. A large part of my career was spent working in the nuclear power industry. Policies and procedures were the basis of operations. Safety was paramount. No excuses tolerated.

If you are an Excuse Conquistador, your friends probably describe you as serious and decisive. You respect and obey rules. You probably prefer implementing to creating when given a choice. Examples of occupations that attract Excuse Conquistadors are pilot and engineer.

Column B: The Situational Excuser

If your highest number is in Column B, you often find yourself saying, "It depends." You direct your anger toward solving problems rather than toward people. You use your energy to find answers, not to offer excuses.

Larry Cole, a former defensive lineman who played in a Super Bowl for the Dallas Cowboys, was asked about a slump he had experienced. He said, "Anyone can have an off decade." If you're a Situational Excuser, you look at the facts and then move on to finding remedies.

George Washington said, "It is better to offer no excuse than a bad one." Like Washington, you use excuses sparingly and think through the implications before you do. Some occupations that interest Situational Excusers are those that involve client development, customer service, or research.

Column C: The Excuse Optimizer

If your highest number is in Column C, you have broad interests and are open to new approaches. You're okay with breaking rules if you think you have a good reason. New approaches appeal to you. You believe in having a "Plan B."

You can identify with this quote from Marilyn Monroe: "Ever notice how 'what the hell' is always the right answer?"

Excuses are sometimes a fallback for you when innovations don't get the results you want. "Let's try it!" is a phrase you often use.

In *Moon Called*, Patricia Briggs wrote the following description of a scene: "The werewolf tossed me against a giant packing crate while I was trying to rescue a frightened young girl who'd been kidnapped by an evil witch and a drug lord." Now that's a creative excuse! Excuse Optimizers are playful and use excuses primarily when they're exploring innovative ideas.

Fields that appeal to Excuse Optimizers include marketing, advertising, and art.

Chapter 2

Examples of Excuses: Use These at Your Own Risk

© Randy Glasbergen
glasbergen.com

"Whenever you're mad at me, visit my
web page. I have a searchable database
of apologies and excuses for every occasion!"

"He that is good for
making excuses is
seldom good for
anything else."

Benjamin Franklin

Excuses with a Purpose

People can be very creative when it comes to excuses – especially when the excuse is a cover for the real message they're not telling you. And some excuses are so outrageous that they become shorthand for a concept – part of the language of the team. Here's an example from my own life.

My parents heard so many excuses over the years from their children for being late that they used an acronym to bypass them. They quit saying "Goodbye" when children left the house. Instead they said "DBL" which stood for "Don't be late." It was shorthand for "Be on time. Don't bother to create an excuse. Just observe the curfew."

People make excuses for not doing something. People also make excuses for things they did. They even take actions – or don't take them – to create an excuse. "I'm not going to clean off my desk so I'll have a reason for not finishing the report today." "If I don't call, then I won't have to deal with rejection."

You might consider recording some of the most memorable or humorous excuses given by team members. You can use them to illustrate how excuses can be a distraction and a barrier.

No book on excuses would be complete without some examples and a few laughs.

Excuses for Being Late to Work

These are actual examples. What is the real message?

- I dropped my purse in a coin operated newspaper box and didn't have change to open it.

- An employee called his boss to say that he would be late for work because of car trouble. When asked what the problem with his car was, he replied, "I'm not in it."

Excuses that Are Delaying Tactics

If you hear these, you know the real message is that something is not going to happen.

- I need a proposal.

- I have to ask for approval.

- Let me check the budget.

- I'll have to present it to the committee.

Excuses to Avoid Doing Something

Be alert for red flags like these excuses.

- It's been done before/already been done/someone else has done it better.

- It's too hard.

- It didn't work last time.

- The timing is bad.

- I don't know how.

- It will take too long.

- I already gave at the office.

- I already do volunteer work.

- That doesn't apply to me.

- I don't feel like it.

- I have too many other things to do.

- It might not be a success.

- I'm not inspired right now.

- The competition is too stiff.

- I never got the message.

- I didn't get the email. It must have gone to the spam folder.

- Someone else hasn't completed his

part and I need it before I can pro-
ceed.

- It isn't my decision.

- My cell phone didn't have service.

- I can't get started.

- I might make a mistake.

- I need to get ready to get ready.

"Two wrongs don't make
a right, but they make a
good excuse."

Thomas Stephen Szasz

Excuses That Are Industry-Specific

The excuses that appear below came from actual insurance claims.* What excuses are common in your work?

- Coming home I drove into the wrong house and collided with a tree I don't have.

- I thought my window was down, but I found it was up when I put my head through it.

- As I approached an intersection a sign suddenly appeared in a place where no stop sign had ever appeared before. I was unable to stop in time to avoid the accident.

- I pulled in to the side of the road because there was smoke coming from under the hood. I realized there was a fire in the engine, so I took my dog and smothered it with a blanket.

- No one was to blame for the accident but it would never have happened if the other driver had been alert.

- The indirect cause of the accident was a little guy in a small car with a big mouth.

- I knew the dog was possessive about the car but I would not have asked her to drive it if I had thought there was any risk.

- The accident happened because I had one eye on the truck in front, one eye on the pedestrian, and the other on the car behind.

* The source for these insurance examples is http://www.swapmeetdave.com/Humor/Insurance/Insurance.htm.

Chapter 3

Causes of Excuses:
Who Knew?

© Randy Glasbergen / glasbergen.com

"We make better apologies and excuses than any
other company in our industry and I'm proud of that!"

"Success is a tale of
obstacles overcome,
and for every obstacle
overcome, an excuse
not used."

Robert Brault

Common Causes of Excuses

Fear is often the underlying reason for making an excuse.

Fear of the unknown. Fear of success. Fear of using up opportunities. Fear of taking a risk.

Other causes include procrastination, difficulty dealing with ambiguity, the desire to buy time, or lack of clarity. Perfectionism. Desire to keep your options open. The culture. Habit. Inertia. Being stuck in old behaviors. Politeness trumping honesty. Personality traits that favor making excuses. Discomfort. Uncertainty. Dislike of closure. Defense of an action taken. Need for harmony. A search for a better alternative. All these often lead to excuses.

There are probably as many reasons for making an excuse as there are members on your team. Getting rid of excuses requires that you understand what is prompting them. What is being rewarded? What do you say to yourself when you make an excuse?

A colleague said he was on a weight reduction program. His associate said, "That's a terrible idea. If you lose weight, you'll wrinkle." The comment wasn't enough to deter him, but it made him pause for a moment. Do excuses flourish in your work group because they are encouraged?

Excuses sometimes are caused by psychological conflict. Approach-approach conflict exists when two alternatives seem equally appealing. Avoidance-avoidance is when you don't embrace either option. Approach-avoidance describes being able to see advantages and disadvantages that have the same weight. Resolve the conflict and you eliminate the tendency to make an excuse.

"Scared isn't a good excuse. Scared is the excuse everyone has always used."

John Green

What's Behind the Excuses in Your Work Group?

Motivation Checklist

Think about a few excuses that you've made or that you've heard. What were they? Why did you or someone else make the excuse? It's been said, "Prescription without diagnosis is malpractice." You can't take steps that will have the long-term effect of preventing excuses unless you identify the causes.

Here are some possible causes for making excuses.

- Denial

- Perfectionism

- Role models and friends use excuses

- Scarcity mentality (If you do something now, you'll use up a resource that will be more valuable later.)

- Desire to please without identifying the real situation

- Discomfort with ambiguity

- Uncertainty about what you want

- Culture makes excuses okay

- Rewards for excuses exist

- Lack of focus

- Wanting to keep options open

- Feeling of helplessness — why bother?

- Urge to take the easy way

- Preference for what is familiar

- Habit

- Defense of an action

- Means of easing discomfort or anxiety

- Strategy for retreating

- Lack of resilience

- Being locked in a set of beliefs

- Procrastination

- Rationalization

- Fear of failure

- Fear of success

- Way to avoid doing something else

When you notice someone else offering an excuse, why do you think they did it? It's important to consider *their* perspective — not why *you* would have done it. Then the problem solving can begin.

Chapter 4

Excuse Zappers: Seven Sure-Fire Strategies

"We've found a role in the company for your special talent. We're promoting you to C.E.O...Chief Excuses Officer."

"Never make excuses. Your friends don't need them and your foes won't believe them."

John Wooden

Strategy #1:

Be Careful Who Your Closest Associates Are

> "You are the average of the five people you spend the most time with."
>
> Jim Rohn

People Audit

David Campbell, an eminent psychologist, once warned, "Be careful who your friends are, you become just like them." The same principle applies to your associates at work.

Who Are the Five People You See the Most?

1.

2.

3.

4.

5.

Ask Yourself These Questions:

- In general, would you say they have a positive, "can do" attitude?

- Do they deliver feedback in a supportive way?

- How deep and wide is their knowledge and experience?

- How frequently do they offer excuses?

- How strong is their desire for you to succeed?

- What is their history as a coach/mentor/cheerleader/supporter of others?

- Are they good role models?

Cultivate Sources of Professional Support

Since your associates have a huge impact on your success, it's wise to find the right ones. Colleagues can be invaluable to help with excuse-prevention. Their attitudes toward excuses are contagious. Who do you choose for lunch dates? Who do you consider a confidant?

If you don't have good sources of professional support, consider starting your own group. I've been in several that provided great feedback. One was a small band of entrepreneurs that met every two weeks for lunch. We called ourselves the Monet Group because we sat at a table under a print by Monet. Members described a challenge they faced, got input, and said what steps they were going to take before the next meeting. Implementing a "Plan B" was okay, but excuses were not.

The second group was a Mastermind Group in which members followed a structured problem-solving model. We shared results, resources, lessons learned, and questions. Each week we used video conferencing tools to meet. Accountability was a key. We dealt in solutions, not excuses.

A third strategy for getting feedback and encouragement from someone who understands the issues you face is to find a trusted sounding board. I discovered another aspiring author who was also struggling with her first book. Excuses for not writing abound for most authors. It's hard to find the discipline to be productive for long stretches of time. And most writers work alone.

First, we listed all the tasks involved and decided to email each other periodic updates. Then we realized that too much time was being spent rationalizing our lack of progress in lengthy messages. So we changed our approach.

We each figured out the target date for publication for our book and estimated how many hours a day it would take to meet the deadline. Because we found that we were spending as much time composing our friendly emails as we were working on our books, we changed the format. We decided to send an email at the end of each day that said, "Did it." The recipient replied some variation of "Great!" We met for "book reports" periodically.

Sometimes the situation is very complex and you might benefit from the advice of an objective listener who can recommend resources. Talking with a business coach can be an effective way to overcome excuses that are barriers to your success.

Select Your Work Group Members Wisely

Surround yourself with the best. It's easier to select for the traits you want than it is to train for them. If you want to choose team members who are optimistic, get things done efficiently, value collaboration, and communicate well, then you should have a process that will enable you to hire people with these capabilities.

The best predictor of future behavior is past behavior. Actual examples of how someone acted in a particular type of situation will yield good data. Ask their references if they've displayed the characteristics you seek. I'd advise developing a standard set of interview questions that will give you an idea if the candidate is excuse-prone.

Sample "excuse" questions include:

- What were the circumstances the last time you made an excuse?

- What do you do when someone you were depending on offers an excuse rather than honoring a commitment?

- How would you go about creating an

excuse-free culture for a work group?

- Do excuses have any value in the workplace?

- Tell me how you handle ambiguity.

Strategy #2:

Learn to Unlearn

> "The most important lessons lay not in what I needed to learn, but in what I first needed to unlearn."
>
> Jim Collins

Unlearning is Critical

What should I do? What's the best course of action? Which direction should I choose? What's holding me back? What occurred in the team's history that might be distorting objectivity?

Sometimes people get so used to old ways of thinking or doing something, that they don't realize they're placing constraints on their options. Excuses come naturally.

Just for a moment, take a look back. What are your habits concerning excuses? What is your team's history of excuses? One high-impact exercise that is used in team building is to post a long piece of paper and create a time line for the team from its launch to the present. Major events, accomplishments, lessons learned, and derailments are captured.

It would be revealing to do this and then ask members to think about the circumstances surrounding the milestones. When there were setbacks, were excuses made? Are there any behaviors surrounding excuses that the team needs to unlearn? Perhaps what worked well in the past won't be effective in the future. Times change. Management philosophies change. Industries change. Maybe excuses were tolerated in the past, but they won't serve the team well in the next business cycle.

Psychologists have observed that the

unlearning curve is frequently steeper than the learning curve. First you have to become aware of what you're doing. Then you have to be motivated to make a change. Then you have to realize that you might be more effective acting in a different way. Next you have to practice and maintain new skills. It's not necessary to abandon what you already know. But you have to make adjustments and add to your repertoire.

Are old habits getting in your way? Without thinking, are you making excuses when they don't take you where you want to go? Are you accepting excuses because politeness is the norm? Identifying the reason why the excuse was made will lead to better results in the future.

Lessons on unlearning can be gleaned from looking at what happens during a merger or acquisition. A lot of them are unsuccessful. It's a time that is ripe for excuses. It's often easier to create an excuse for not doing something than it is to change. If your team is operating in uncertain circumstances, be aware that people may hold on to the old way of doing things because it feels safe. They make excuses for not embracing new approaches. This happens especially when people have a sense of loss.

William Bridges, in his book *Transitions*, points out that endings and new beginnings aren't the hardest periods of adjustment. He describes the period in-between as being comparable to Moses in the wilderness after he left Egypt and before he saw the Promised Land. He also compared it to what Linus in *Peanuts* must feel when his blanket is in the dryer. Be aware of you team's environment. Excuses may flourish during times of transition.

How do customary ways of doing things get in your way or impede the progress of your team? When conducting a workshop for a struggling new executive team of a merged business, I asked each participant what was the last change they made - either personally or as a leader.

Some of the reasons they were struggling became apparent when members realized that they don't make changes easily. Without exception, they each went to the same place at the same time for vacation. None liked trying different restaurants or types of food. Plenty of similar examples existed in their business lives. And making an excuse was their first reaction when they faced ambiguity.

As a leader, if you notice that excuses are increasing, ask yourself if there's any information you can provide that will increase comfort when associates risk using new behavior. Some people use ceremonies such as throwing away keys to former offices to help them abandon excuses and let go of the old. Most find it easiest to "unlearn" if they identify and celebrate taking small steps. Be aware that excuses can be a signal that transition plans may need to be revised. Don't let old habits or assumptions get in the way of rapid progress.

What's your exit strategy from harmful excuses for you and your team? It may be useful to think of what you want to accomplish and what you have to leave behind to get there. Remember that going somewhere means you have to leave somewhere else.

> ## "Man cannot discover new oceans unless he has the courage to lose sight of the shore."
>
> ### André Gide

Are excuses preventing you from making new discoveries? Do old habits interfere with having courage to explore the unknown and learn new skills?

In his famous ballad "The Gambler," Kenny Rogers sings, "You got to know when to hold 'em, know when to fold 'em, know when to walk away and know when to run." When you're launching a new initiative, it's time to run from excuses.

Strategy #3:

Realize That There is No "Try"

> "No! Try not. Do, or do not. There is no try."
>
> Yoda

An Excuse-Free Zone

Yoda, a character in the movie *Star Wars — The Empire Strikes Back*, made that memorable comment. In an excuse-free culture it is certainly true. Words — especially excuses — don't count. Only results do.

Back in elementary school, teachers used to give grades for effort. In business, particularly in start-ups, effort isn't relevant and excuses aren't tolerated.

Conduct this experiment and see what happens. Get agreement from team members that any time someone makes an excuse, he or she will put a dollar in a prominently displayed jar. No exceptions. The recognition of the excuse focuses attention on behaviors that get in the way of effectiveness and efficiency. And it serves as a deterrent for everyone.

An instructor in a sales training class fined participants every time they said the word "try." Each occurrence in a sentence counted. Every setting was monitored. Coffee breaks, the parking lot, and the classroom were all observed. The technique was remarkably effective. People policed their own language and that of others. Humor was rampant and softened the blow of making a mistake. At first, tallies were kept and records for frequency were established. Then the word, and its synonyms, vanished from everyone's vocabulary. Keeping track of excuses will have the same effect. They'll begin to disappear.

When you hear the words, "I tried," what's your reaction? You probably think something like, "But not hard enough." Or you wonder why the person didn't persist. Or perhaps you wonder if any real attempt was made at all. Making an effort isn't a good excuse when others are depending on you or when the results are important. Do it. Excuses are not acceptable. Being aware of them will make you successful faster.

"Do not make excuses, whether it's your fault or not."

George S. Patton, Jr

Strategy #4:

Pay Attention to the Power of Language

"Let's eat, Grandmother.
Let's eat Grandmother."

Unknown

Words Matter

I've seen the above quote on a t-shirt with the subscript, "Commas save lives." One missing comma changes the entire meaning of the statement. How many excuses are made because of misunderstandings? Because you really didn't understand the situation and the consequences?

Before automatically giving an excuse, try saying, "This is too important for me to risk not understanding. Let me say it back to you." Repeat what you think you heard. Then you can choose the best course of action.

There's a world of difference between "Let's eat, grandmother," and "Let's eat grandmother." Are you making excuses because the idea wasn't presented clearly and it's more expedient to say "no" than it is to explore what was really said?

Differences in speaking styles and listening styles cause lots of misunderstandings. Is the listener distracted? Do idioms interfere with communication? Afferbeck Lauder wrote *Let's Talk Strine* and Steve Mitchell is the author of *How to Speak Southern*. They are both humorous looks at how language leads to confusion. Customary ways of speaking can also lead to misunderstandings about excuses. An example of a regional difference is that Northerners often don't realize that Southerners aren't really making an excuse when they decline a request. They're waiting to hear it a second time to make sure it's real.

For example, a Southerner is apt to say, "No, thank you." if someone offers to go the grocery store for them when they're sick. If the suggestion is made a second time with words like, "I'm going to run errands. What can I get you?" it will probably be gratefully accepted.

I enjoy having lots of company at my beach cottage. The washing machine is old, is located on the second floor, and doesn't have a pan underneath it. As a precautionary measure, I turn off the water when the machine is not in use. On the washing machine, there is a prominently displayed sign that says, "Turn on the water before starting the machine. Turn it off after machine has finished." That way, I don't have to worry about leaks.

Recently, a guest decided to wash clothes and I heard an ominous buzzing sound. I asked if she had turned on the water and she replied, "I didn't think that sign applied to me."

Just when you think that your language couldn't be any clearer, people surprise you. The lesson I learned is that, even when you think no one could miss the point, someone does. Checking for understanding is never a bad idea when it's important. And it prevents excuses.

Strategy #5:

Perform an Excuse Audit

> "If you really want to do something, you'll find a way. If you don't, you'll find an excuse."
>
> Jim Rohn

The Excuse Audit

Many lessons about excuse management can be learned from observing people in helping professions. For example, a particularly effective dental technician always asks patients, "What stops you from flossing regularly?" instead of saying, "You should floss more often." She then uses the information they provide to help them change their behavior. A good psychotherapist poses excellent questions rather than giving answers. He enables clients to get clarity for themselves and determine steps they need to take. A well-respected dance instructor was described not as criticizing students but showing the way. The tone used and the questions asked eliminated defensiveness and the tendency to reach for an excuse.

Feedback has been described as the breakfast of champions. It's certainly true that feedback is a gift. Without data, how would you know if you're effective? Sometimes it's hard to assess the impact you have on others - especially if they are editing their words because you're their boss. Often leaders get trapped in old habits without being aware that they aren't choosing their words well.

Excuse Audit Questions

Directions: Ask yourself the following questions before you make excuses. Do a quick evaluation by answering "Yes" or "No."

_____ 1. Are there long-range consequences?

_____ 2. Are my words compatible with my values?

_____ 3. Will making an excuse help me get to where I want to be?

_____ 4. Will l ever have this opportunity again?

_____ 5. Could I be doing something else that would be better?

_____ 6. Is the excuse just the easy way out?

_____ 7. Is it likely that I'll regret giving this excuse?

_____ 8. Will an excuse take care of the

situation or just delay dealing with it?

_____ 9. Will the excuse have a negative impact on my reputation?

_____ 10. Am I making an excuse to avoid getting out of my comfort zone?

Now ask yourself: "Should I make the excuse?"

Strategy #6:

Leverage Strengths

"I tried for a whole summer to teach our cat to play the piano. We started with an easy song. It was 3 Blind Mice. My dad said it didn't work because the cat had a tin ear, but I think it was because she kept looking around for the blind mice the whole time and never gave it her full attention."

Brian Andreas, Story People

Story People capture wonderful, whimsical perspectives on everyday events and publish them in books and prints. This is one of my favorites. It's a good example of the power of understanding strengths.

Can't you imagine the cat saying things like, "I'm too busy to practice." Or, "I lost my sheet music." Or, "I have to go chase birds right now." Excuse after excuse. The cat would say anything that would prevent it from having to take piano lessons. The job requirements didn't match the capabilities.

Leadership success depends upon identifying skill sets and capitalizing on them. When responsibilities are assigned without doing an analysis of the potential for success, excuses are used as a defense mechanism. Why attempt something when failure is inevitable? Excuses serve the purpose of avoiding negative consequences.

I saw this quote on a button: "If it's out of reach, s-t-r-e-t-c-h." Research shows that people try hardest when they have a

50-50 chance of achieving a goal. If there is no possibility whatsoever, why spend the effort? If there is no element of challenge, why bother to give it your all? You already know the results will be acceptable, if not great.

An assessment of strengths is the foundation of a no-excuse culture. Have you taken an inventory of your own strengths recently? There are many techniques for doing this – from taking sophisticated psychological tests to using a series of simple questions.

There are three quick and easy ways to update your own strengths inventory. The first is to ask yourself what you do that gets compliments. Another is to keep track of the types of advice that colleagues request from you. What strengths are they asking you to share? The third is to make a list of 50 things you do well.

Fifty may seem like a lot. But if you make yourself write down a large number, you force yourself to look beyond the recent past. When I've given similar instructions to workshop participants, they usually can think of at least 25 in three minutes. Are you willing to spend a few minutes to be successful fast and to eliminate excuses?

Sometimes a real reason can sound like an excuse. Are you able to list the top five strengths of each of your team members? Taken as a whole, what are your work group's strengths? You get optimum productivity, satisfaction, and motivation when assignments match strengths. Then there's no need for excuses. People flourish.

What distinguishes great leaders from average ones? It's their ability to remove the need to make excuses by assigning responsibilities based upon abilities. Outstanding leaders recognize strengths, nurture potential, and eliminate distracting excuses.

Strategy #7:

Banish Blame

"People are always blaming their circumstances for what they are. I don't believe in circumstances. The people who get on in this world are the people who get up and look for the circumstances they want, and, if they can't find them, make them."

George Bernard Shaw

Never, Ever Blame

At a workshop I attended, an instructor asked participants to think of the worst thing that had happened to them and tell the person sitting next to them about it. As a member of the audience, all I could think was, "Sure. I'm never going to do that!" Sharing something awful with a stranger sounded like a bad idea and had no appeal to me. But the point the facilitator was trying to make was relevant to excuses. After the participants shared what happened, he asked them to then identify their role in the event. No matter how terrible, he suggested there must be some aspect that they might have controlled.

When you hear an excuse, ask yourself, "What was my role in prompting it?" If you start to blame someone else as an excuse, figure out if you had a role. Did you make a request too late? Did the person have the resources or capabilities required?

Blaming someone or something as an

excuse is bad form. As a leader, it makes you look powerless. It leads to lack of trust and loss of goodwill.

Reinhold Niebuhr's famous serenity prayer, "God, grant me the serenity to accept the things I cannot change, the courage to change the things I can, and wisdom to know the difference," can also apply to excuses. Know the difference between a flimsy excuse and a real reason. Be willing to help change excuses into constructive actions when the situation can and should be altered.

The famous quote by Benjamin Disraeli, "Never complain and never explain," could be expanded to include "and never blame."

And the military leader George S. Patton, Jr. said, "Do not make excuses, whether it's your fault or not." Good leaders banish blame.

Chapter 5

Excuse Busters:
Mission and Goals

Manifest excellence beyond a paradigm of
betterment with magnitude for implementation
of probity and cohesion with coalescence and
diversity of purpose steadfast, bounded only
by our prescience and predestination as we
gloriously emanate eminence for the divine
unified triumph toward quintessential destiny!

GLASBERGEN

"I'm not satisfied with the new mission statement.
I can still understand parts of it."

"There's a difference between interest and commitment. When you're interested in doing something, you do it only when it's convenient. When you're committed to something, you accept no excuses - only results."

Kenneth H. Blanchard

Involvement vs. Commitment

There's an old fable of a pig and a chicken. The chicken is recommending that someone have a breakfast of ham and eggs. The pig remarks: "That's easy for you to say. You'd only be involved. I'd have to show real commitment."

Excuses multiply when there is involvement rather than commitment. And it's hard to be committed when you're unsure of the goal.

You're not even in the game yet if you don't know what the overall goal is, plus the part you're to play in reaching it. You don't have any basis for crafting a course of action or for evaluating alternatives.

Goal clarity is the price of admission. And it's essential for creating an excuse-free culture. Otherwise, it's possible to offer excuses without thinking or bothering to ask yourself if you're making the right decision.

> "A small body of determined spirits fired by an unquenchable faith in their mission can alter the course of history."

Mahatma Gandhi

How to Get Clarity and Alignment

When facilitating workshops to help teams jump-start success, I ask each participant to write the mission of the team on a piece of flip chart paper and tape it up on the wall. This exercise is such an eye opener! Each participant's mission is usually completely different from all the others - and very different than the team leader's version.

The lack of clarity about why the group exists leads to missteps, wasted effort, demoralization, and lots of excuses. Team members want to do a good job, but their individual priorities don't support the big goals. They don't know what the mission is or the implications for carrying out their responsibilities. When asked, "Why did you do that?" the reasons they give sound like excuses. Their good intentions were sabotaged by the leader's failure to ensure everyone understood the mission as well as their individual responsibilities.

Two complaints I often hear when talking with teams and boards are, "No one ever told me," and "No one ever asked me." This simple workshop exercise accomplishes both. It's a way to get alignment of objectives and a way to get input. Excuses evaporate when everyone has clarity about the team's mission.

Chapter 6

Excuse Recognition: Weasel Spotting and Other Applications

© Randy Glasbergen
glasbergen.com

"Heads — better customer service.
Tails — better excuses!"

"If you don't want to do something, one excuse is as good as another."

Yiddish Proverb

Red Flags

What are the red flags in your environment that indicate you're probably going to hear excuses from some team members for not honoring their commitments? Are you paying attention to them?

He's Just Not That Into You: The No-Excuses Truth to Understanding Guys by Greg Behrendt and Liz Tuccillo is a guide to red flags in dating relationships. Their message applies to the business environment as well: "Consider the perspective of the other person. Denial will not serve you well."

In their research on executive competencies, Bob Echinger and Michael Lombardo found an important characteristic of great leaders. It was the ability to learn quickly from experience. Make sure you're paying attention. The difference between having five years of experience and one year's experience five times is the skill of noticing danger signs the first time they appear.

Your experience is your direct experience as a leader, your observations of others, and your years interacting with internal or external clients. What have you learned are the red flags that lead to excuses and broken promises? What can you do to be proactive and avert them? Unexpected excuses cost you time, money, stress, and lost opportunities.

Serious red flags in the form of verbal and non-verbal excuses abound in the workplace. It always amazes me that some people are so oblivious to them.

As manager of an outplacement center, I heard lots of examples of these red flags from my clients who had lost their jobs. Some stories seemed more like messages in neon lights than red flags. Yet people ignored them – often losing their jobs.

One of the most common cues is being excluded from meetings or decision-making. Here's an incident that should have been a sign to take corrective action immediately. An employee was told to show up for a meeting at 9:00 a.m. When the employee arrived on time, people were leaving. When he asked why, he was told, "Everyone was here by 8:30 so we started early." No apology. No other reasons given. No offers were made to fill him in on what happened. Yet he was surprised when he discovered that his job was in danger. The serious red flag was him not hearing the excuse.

Office doors that are frequently closed are another indication that all is not well. That's a common sign of job jeopardy if no excuses are offered.

Hearing the same excuse more than once is another serious red flag. Being told "Timing is everything," over and over can mean that, to top management, your proposed idea doesn't have any appeal to them and never will.

Common business wisdom is that if you do something right and don't hear about it, that's normal. If you do something wrong and don't hear about it, update your resume. No excuse can save you.

Woody Allen once said in an interview,

"Eighty percent of success is showing up." If you interpret "showing up" to include being sensitive to the use of excuses, his advice certainly applies to the workplace.

In an era of layoffs, paying attention to excuses – and the lack of them – can provide clues to your job security and chances of promotion. The surest way to do well is to be aware of the excuses in your environment and to avoid making them yourself. The best way to be a great leader is to be straightforward and not hide behind excuses. Ever.

Excuse Prevention in Special Settings

When discussing challenges that businesses face, an entrepreneur described a problem that was costing him time and money. He lends money to new ventures and puts together financial partnerships. He said he was often surprised by clients who are good financial risks, who fill out lots of paperwork on their background, and who put down earnest money and sound enthusiastic about a project. Everything is "good to go." Then they back out at the last minute – even if it means forfeiting a large deposit. Their excuses are flimsy or nonexistent.

Another executive said that his organization was facing a "yield problem." Despite making the effort to pre-qualify applicants, marketing efforts were not yielding paying customers. Potential clients go to the trouble of filling out an extensive application to enroll in a therapy program that has a 40-year track record of success. It produces results that last a lifetime after a two-week investment of time. People fill out the application and choose a date. Then they don't show up.

Sales reps report the same thing happens to them all the time. Despite having qualified a client.

When I mentioned this problem to a banker who deals with a lot of loan applications, he said, "Oh, you're studying weasels." How can you protect yourself from weasels in business and in your personal life? How do you prevent yourself from deserving the label?

The famous social psychologist, Kurt Lewin, described a phenomenon called approach-avoidance conflict that may help explain weasels' actions. It's a source of stress when a goal or event has both negative and positive consequences that are of equal value in the decision maker's mind, and he can choose only one or the other. For example, the financial dealmaker is attracted to the prospect of making money but is deterred by the risk involved. Maybe he discovered new data, creating approach-avoidance conflict, as the deadline for finalizing the contract approached.

A beautiful botanical garden attracts enthusiastic volunteers with sought-after skills. The director depends on them for special events, fundraising, and website development. All is well until they have an opportunity to use their day doing something they would enjoy more.

A large art museum uses volunteers to fill positions and free up the time of paid staff for more complex tasks. It works fine until a volunteer is late or doesn't show up - using the excuse, "I'm just a volunteer."

How do you avoid weasels? You can make one choice more appealing than the other. Or you can provide a positive consequence for following through and a negative one for not doing what was promised. For example, offering a discount or giving public recognition would be a positive consequence. While having to pay a financial penalty or not receiving an invitation to a special event would be a negative one.

And it always helps to make expectations crystal clear from the very beginning.

"Shoot low, boys. They're ridin' Shetland ponies."

Lewis Grizzard

Lewis Grizzard's words of advice come in handy when you're involved in weasel spotting. They're a reminder to know your audience. Pay attention to red flags. Realize that your client's perspective may be, and probably is, different from yours.

Most people operate from the point of view of "What's in it for me?" It's so common that WIIFM has become part of everyday conversation. Yet it's easy to forget that your client, your associate, your prospective customer, or the volunteer at your organization may be operating from a framework that is totally different from yours. Hit your target and get the results you want by thinking about what they really want.

Chapter 7

Leadership and Excuses: Straightforward Secrets of Success

"What fits your busy schedule better, exercising one hour a day or being dead 24 hours a day?"

"One of the most impor-
tant tasks of a manager is
to eliminate his people's
excuses for failure."

Robert Townsend

Importance of Culture

In 1519, Spanish Conquistador Hernando Cortez landed on the Yucatan Peninsula with 11 ships containing 500 soldiers and 100 sailors. His objective was to seize the riches of the Aztecs. He raised the motivation of his troops by accepting no excuses for failure. His famous words that ensured total commitment were, "Burn the ships!" His own ships. He said, "If we are going home, we are going home in their ships." It was do or die. Failure was not an option. Excuses were out of the question.

Are you, as a leader, leaving the door open for doubts about your commitment to the group's goals? Are you providing back-ups that can be used as excuses? How do you rate as an excuse manager?

One way to make sure that you are doing an excellent job of removing obstacles to success for your work group is to ask for feedback. A colleague used an effective strategy when he was preparing for a job interview that you can easily adapt.

He asked several of his associates to list at least three things he did well so he could highlight them when talking to his prospective boss. It's a lot less threatening than to ask for examples of mistakes. What would your team members say if you asked them to name the actions you have taken to remove excuses? If they can't think of any, consider it a wake-up call.

In the movie *It's a Wonderful Life*, every time an angel gets its wings, a bell rings. Every time you make an excuse, an alarm should go off in your mind. Why did you do that? What does the excuse really mean to your team?

Do they have the resources they need? What's the culture you have created? Do you have an open-door policy? Do you inspire trust? What do you reward? What's your reputation?

If you learn that people perceive you as always being late, backing out at the last minute, or using excuses, it's time to make changes.

Power of Role Models

A successful manager spoke about the keys to his achievements at a leadership conference. He said that he always looked around for the best role model and used those behaviors as his standard. Not the person who came in late, or had excuses for missed deadlines, or did the minimum. But the one with the great attitude, with the respect of fellow workers, and with a reputation for excellence. He'd observed that many new associates unthinkingly follow bad examples. Who are your role models? Do they make excuses? Are you a good role model?

> "If you accept excuses from others, it's usually because you have accepted your own excuse."
>
> Orrin Woodward

A male manager once told the story of staying in a hotel that had a mirror in the bathroom that had 10x magnification. He looked in it and was shocked. His asked himself, "Why would anyone want to use this?" Once he got over his surprise, he saw the value of having more data about himself.

That's the purpose of the questions below. If you're not the excuse-free leader you'd like to be, you will have specific information on what changes to make. What gets measured gets done. What gets rewarded happens again. Examples influence behavior.

- How do excuses affect your team?

- What three words do you think your colleagues use to describe your leadership style when you're not around?

- Is "reliable" part of your reputation?

- If your staff were to identify an ideal

role model for excuse management, would they name you?

- Do your associates make excuses for you such as, "He's so busy," or "She's under stress," or "He's just got a lot on his mind?"

- What's the bottom line when it comes to the frequency and impact of your own excuses?

- How do you react when someone makes an excuse?

- How would you like your team members to describe the excuse culture of your work group?

Chapter 8

The Good Excuse: There is an Exception to Every Rule

"The key to office politics is to let others share credit for your work...especially when you fail."

"It is better to offer no excuse than a bad one."

George Washington

Excuse Etiquette

When nothing else will do and you have to make an excuse to spare someone's feelings, or to buy time to think, or to avoid a dire consequence, there are principles to keep in mind to limit the damage.

- Keep it short.

- Don't provide details.

- Make sure you don't get caught telling an untruth.

- Remember what you said.

- Avoid using the same excuse too often.

- Realize that there may be undesired consequences.

- Protect your reputation by rarely using excuses.

- Be sensitive to the needs and personality of the listener.

- Recognize that, if you have to make an excuse, you need to do it sooner rather than later.

- Don't blame someone else.

- Offer an alternative.

- Tell the truth even if you have to limit your excuse to, "I'm sorry I can't do it."

- Know that sometimes an excuse is not acceptable.

- Treat others as you'd like them to treat you.

> ## "I must decline your invitation owing to a subsequent invitation."
>
> Oscar Wilde

Whatever you say, make every effort to avoid having a quote like this one from Oscar Wilde attributed to you.

When to Make an Excuse

Sometimes an excuse serves as the equivalent of a white lie. You make an excuse to spare the feelings of someone else - usually in social situations. But sometimes it's necessary in business as well.

My very polite, extremely ladylike mother once said, by mistake, in response to a dinner invitation from someone she didn't particularly like, "I couldn't come even if I wanted to." Fortunately I overheard her telephone conversation and asked her if she knew what she just said. She was mortified. She immediately called back and made not one but two excuses. The first was a reason she invented that got her off the hook for her comment. The second one was a sincere sounding description of a conflict that prevented her from accepting.

"Traffic is very heavy at the moment, so if you are thinking of leaving now, you'd better set off a few minutes earlier."

Anonymous Traffic Report

It might seem like an obvious thing to say, but be aware of your own words before you say them. Be sure to edit if you're in a situation where you care about the impact.

A friend described a situation that clearly called for an excuse. When she asked another person if she would like a ride to a birthday party, she got the answer, "I'm not going because I don't want to honor the person having a birthday." This was an instance where offering an excuse would have spared feelings. Even a lukewarm equivalent of the old joke, "I can't go because I have to wash my hair," would have shown better manners and sensitivity.

Less is more. Consider your audience and put them ahead of yourself. Think about the consequences of your words.

A new employee was still in a probationary period with an organization that had a strict policy concerning all drugs - prescription and nonprescription. She had listed all of her medications on her application. During the first days on the job, she couldn't sleep at night. She took an Ambien out of her sister's medicine cabinet and swallowed it without thinking. The next morning she was groggy and realized that she might have jeopardized her job. Only after she had phoned her supervisor and said that she wasn't coming in that day because she took a sleeping pill, she realized that a more general excuse might have served her better until she'd established a track record as a drug-free, reliable, high performer. "I'm not feeling well," would have been a truthful excuse and a better choice of words.

Know the listener. Take into account your objective. Be truthful, but choose your words well. Emotional intelligence counts when it comes to making excuses. The best option is not to do anything that requires one.

Excuses as Gifts

When I first started writing this book, the topic was "how to harness the power of excuses." People kept saying that they didn't understand how that could be the focus of a book because it implied that excuses were okay. While they're not inherently good, they can be useful. Think of an excuse as an opportunity to learn - about yourself or about someone else. What is really being said?

If you look at the excuses that you make to others, they can be sources of information about what you really want to do and they provide information about your relationships.

If you probe the excuses customers or potential clients make, you are conducting market research. You discover how you can improve.

As I mentioned earlier, feedback is called the breakfast of champions. You may have noticed that the heading on the comment cards many businesses ask customers to complete says, "Feedback is a gift." It's an invaluable present when you want to enhance performance.

Listen to the excuses of your clients and potential clients. What does the information tell you? Is there a pattern to the excuses? When you hear the same excuse more than once, instead of being upset with the person who made it, think of it as data you can use to improve performance. Do you need to provide more resources? More information? Longer deadlines?

In training films, John Cleese used to tell the story of Gordon the Guided Missile that he remembered from his childhood. He shared that missiles don't take a straight route to their target. They make thousands of course corrections as they fly. The path to excellence is not linear. Excuses provide data you can use to make changes so you won't land short of your goal.

Chapter 9

Implementation of an Anti-Excuse Strategy: The Road to Rapid Results

"What do we make where I work? Mostly we make excuses."

"At the end of the day, let there be no excuses, no explanations, no regrets."

Steve Maraboli

AhMo

"AhMo." Say it out loud. (Aaaaah Moe.) It's been the battle cry of Wylie High School in North Texas since the 1970's. It's used in the context of "Ahmo" going to do something big. What's your "AhMo?" What are you going to do? What well thought-out steps are you going to take today to manage excuses? Tomorrow? Next week? No more "just didn't do it" for you or your future. No more avoiding tough situations just because they are difficult.

AhMo going to show the others the right way to manage excuses. AhMo going to create an excuse-free culture by implementing the following steps:

- Figure out what I should be doing and what I shouldn't be doing

- Look at my own excuse style and propensities

- Notice the most commonly used excuses and eliminate them

- Identify the reasons behind an excuse so I can eradicate the causes

- Use excuse-zappers

    Be careful who my associates are

    Learn to unlearn

    Realize that there is no "try"

    Pay attention to the power of language

    Perform an excuse audit

    Leverage strengths

    Banish blame

- Make sure that the mission and goals are clear to everyone

- Be aware of red flags that signal an excuse is imminent

- Create leadership strategies that prevent excuses

- Know how to make a good excuse when there is no acceptable alternative

- Share *Wouldacouldashoulda* principles with my work group and help make them norms.

Just as with any behavior change, it's a good idea to figure out how to make incremental progress. Psychologists use the practice of successive approximation to help people learn. They identify goals and then identify what it takes to get there – celebrating progress along the way. You're making a commitment to eliminate obstacles to success that appear in the form of excuses. You're saying you want to streamline communication, eliminate misunderstandings, enable associates to focus their energy, get rid of regrets, and take action that will open doors to more and better opportunities.

Leaders know that what gets measured gets done. Just by helping your work group have an awareness of how excuses can derail progress is the first step. The second step is to get buy-in from the whole team that excuses should be banished. There's a big advantage to setting the stage on the first day you become the team leader. The launch of a new initiative is another good chance to create and take steps to maintain an excuse-free zone.

Three Choices

"You've only got three choices in life: Give up, give in, or give it all you've got."

Unknown

What would you like for your group to accomplish in the next six months? In the next year? Capture excuses. Explore the causes. Remember that attitudes toward excuses are contagious. Expect to be wildly successful.

What would Dr. Seuss say to a business leader like you? "You're off to great places, today is your day. Your mountain is waiting so get on your way."

Overcome wouldacouldashouldas and you'll be unstoppable.

Acknowledgments:
Many, Many Thanks

Now I understand why it's almost impossible for recipients of Academy Awards to write great speeches. Fear of forgetting to thank the most important people is paralyzing. There aren't enough pages in this book to hold the names of all those I would like to acknowledge.

The book would not have been possible without my incredible coaches, Geoffrey Berwind, Hal Dibner, and Martha Bullen. My book buddies Gloria Thomas, Tom Davidson, and Laura Carter have been by my side with excellent advice from the very beginning.

My editor, Rhonda J. Fleming, and my designer, Deana Riddle, made invaluable contributions.

Anne Rudgard Royer, Catherine and Glenn Vanderspiegel, Marion Macdonald, and Insiders, thank you for listening and listening and listening.

Tiaras, Hungry Minds, Ah-Ha Group, Sustainer Book Club, and Presidents and Managers, thank you for being my sounding board, for your insightful feedback, and for your unflagging encouragement.

I truly appreciate all that my wonderful friends have done. I wish space constraints didn't limit me to saying, "You know who you are. Thank you from the bottom of my heart for helping me flourish."

Additional Resources:
Paving the Way to a
No-Excuse Zone

Quantity Discounts and Customized Versions

Wouldacouldashoulda: Rapid Results. No Excuses. is available at quantity discounts. Executives benefit from providing each team member a copy when they assume responsibility for a new group or become the leader of an existing one. First-time leaders use it to introduce their expectations. It's valuable as a handout for new team members to help them quickly understand group norms. Companies use customized versions to enhance relationships with their customers and their suppliers. Clients distribute it as an integral part of their new employee orientation sessions.

Workshops

Wouldacouldashoulda: Rapid Results. No Excuses. shows how to help a team flourish. It contains exercises, quizzes, and suggestions that leaders can use on their own and with their employees, colleagues or fellow board members. In addition, Dr. Margaret Bradley offers team development workshops that provide in-depth insights into individual and team strengths, result in tailored action plans, and establish norms that enhance both energy and results. Her transition workshops help leaders obtain faster start-up times and maintain great morale.

Speeches

Are you looking for a speaker who is engaging, entertaining, and focuses on practical, easy-to-implement ways to accelerate incredible outcomes? Tens of thousands of participants have reported success when they applied the principles in Dr. Bradley's presentations.

"Wouldacouldashoulda: Lose the Excuses and Become Wildly Successful Fast" provides insights into the causes of excuses and how to prevent them. Listeners identify their own excuse style and learn how to use practical, no-cost strategies to zap excuses that get in the way of achieving extraordinary outcomes.

"No More Wouldacouldashoulda: What Do You Really Want to Do Now that You've Grown Up?" appeals to professionals who are making – or considering – career transitions. Whether it's accepting a new position, thinking about a different career, joining the workforce, or planning for retirement, information in this speech helps listeners make smooth and regret-free changes.

"Create and Maintain Great Work Relationships" enhances an understanding and appreciation of differences in work styles and communication preferences. This speech leads to reduced stress, increased efficiency, and greater productivity. Audiences learn how to become more effective when cultivating clients, contributing to team goals, and interacting with colleagues.

Contact Information

For information on how to obtain additional copies or customized versions of the book or information about workshops or presentations, please go to www.bradleygroupva.com.

About the Author

Margaret Rudgard Bradley, Ph.D., is an organizational psychologist who has spent her career helping professionals achieve extraordinary results. Her background is an unusual blend of experience as an entrepreneur, a board member, and a manager in large corporations.

Dr. Bradley is known as a practical psychologist who presents serious, complex concepts in an engaging, memorable way. Executives contact her when they need excellent outcomes under tight deadlines.

Her desire to help leaders succeed when they face changing conditions stems from her years of being new to organizations and settings. Dr. Bradley enjoyed life as a member of a Navy family that moved every two years, attended five universities, lived in 31 places before she was 34 years old, held managerial positions in three industries, and has worked with clients ranging from small law firms to corporate giants.

She nurtured her love of learning while earning a Ph.D. from the University of Virginia with 36 hours in the M.B.A. program at the Darden School and a B.A. from Hollins University. She has presented speeches and workshops to tens of thousands of people throughout the U.S. and receives excellent feedback from her audience and workshop attendees.

Dr. Bradley is an ardent fan of anything nautical, everything British, outdoor art shows, mystery novels, innovation, and laughter. She is based in Virginia.

Made in the
USA
Columbia, SC

79963471R00098